WHAT DOG ARE YOU?

Discovering Your Inner Pooch

LORI LEBDA & TAMI BERGESON

WingSpan Press

Copyright © 2007 by Lori Lebda & Tami Bergeson
All rights reserved.

No part of this book may be used or reproduced in any manner without written permission of the author, except for brief quotations used in reviews and critiques.

Printed in the United States of America

Published by WingSpan Press, Livermore, CA
www.wingspanpress.com

The WingSpan name, logo and colophon are the trademarks of WingSpan Publishing.

ISBN 978-1-59594-174-9

First edition 2007

Library of Congress Control Number 2007930364

Lori…For my mom, thanks for always being there, love you. Also, in remembrance of my four legged friends Lonnie, Fritzi, Smokey, Taffy, Pooh Bear, Digger and Scottie.

Tami…For my girls, may you achieve all you dream of. For all of the canine best friends who are on the other side -
- Tramp, Duke, Jenny, Dakota, Gypsy, Shadow, Niki, Duchess (ooie) and Heidi.

WHAT DOG ARE YOU?

Table of Contents

Introduction: The Big YIP! i

Quiz 1: Pooch-Onality 1

Quiz 2: Dapper Dogs 8

Quiz 3: Biscuits or Bones 15

Leader of The Pack: Score List 22

Top Dog: Overall Breed 26

The Kennel: Who's In Your Pack 31

Puppy Love: What's Your Sign 38

Ca-NINE: How Old Are You 45

Purebred Pictures: Find your Photo 48

100 Dogs: Breed Summaries 59

Paws Together: Prayer 74

INTRODUCTION

The Big YIP!

Calling all dog lovers! If you have great affection for the canine species, you're not alone. From the earliest Egyptian days, through the Middle Ages, and numerous worldwide wars until today dogs have been mans best friend and loyal companion. With dozens of breeds out there, which dog are you?

Are you just now getting regular exercise because you're walking your dog? When you leave the house is the television turned up with the Animal Planet channel on? Have you fetched for your dog recently? When we realized that we are the "pets" in our households, we were inspired to write this book.

Answer questions in the following categories: Pooch-Onality, Dapper Dogs, and Biscuits or Bones. Each A, B, C, D, and Yes answers will have a point value. Total your points and then match that number to one out of 100 different dog breeds. After you have taken all three quizzes, combine the scores and match that number to an overall dog. Will you end up as a mixed, half-breed, or purebred? Take the quizzes again another day. Will you be the same dog/dogs? What will your family and friends be? Let's get started.

Quiz 1: POOCH-ONALITY

Grab a pencil, keep score and answer the following personality questions. Match your total points to a dog breed in **Leader of The Pack**. Let's get started and see which dog shares your personality quirks.

A's are worth 10 points.

B's are worth 20 points.

C's are worth 30 points.

D's are worth 40 points.

Yes' are worth 500 points.

No's are worth 0.

1. You have enough energy to ...

    __ A. Shh...ask me later, Scooby's on right now.

    __ B. Find the bone you lost yesterday.

    __ C. Hunt down supper.

    __ D. Traverse a thousand miles to get home.

What Dog Are You? Discovering Your Inner Pooch

2. Are you high-strung when not working?

    __ Yes

    __ No

3. Your weekly exercise schedule is ...

    __ A. Ambling from the bed to a sunny spot.

    __ B. Playing Frisbee a few times.

    __ C. Making several daily laps around my dog run.

    __ D. Constant vigilance around the perimeter of the house.

4. What's your favorite type of game?

    __ A. It's my squeaky. Hands off!

    __ B. Okay, you can throw my bone this once.

    __ C. A play date with a few of my best hounds.

    __ D. A night at the dog park.

5. Pick your favorite physical activity ...

Napping on the porch?

    __ Yes

    __ No

Or, playing fetch?

___ Yes

___ No

Or, going for a long jog?

___ Yes

___ No

Or, training for your next rescue mission?

___ Yes

___ No

6. **Your owner put a quarter in an arcade love-meter machine for you. Would the arrow most likely land on ...**

___ A. Zero-the dud.

___ B. The number three or four-love bug.

___ C. The number six or seven-passionate.

___ D. Eight, nine, ten-Ready or not, here I come!

7. **Would you stray down a dark alley alone?**

___ Yes

___ No

What Dog Are You? Discovering Your Inner Pooch

8. How well do you like other people's pets?

    _ A. I just ignore them.

    _ B. They're okay.

    _ C. I'll play with them for a while.

    _ D. Do they have to leave?

9. Are you independent?

    _ Yes

    _ No

10. You're twentieth in line at the dog wash. Do you...

    _ A. Demand to go home.

    _ B. Sniff the dog in front or behind you.

    _ C. Casually chat with the dogs around you.

    _ D. Have everyone in line form a new playgroup.

11. If left in the wilderness can you find your way home?

    _ Yes

    _ No

12. **Are you a quick study?**

    __ A. What?

    __ B. Smart enough NOT to drink from the toilet.

    __ C. Sure, got the treat?

    __ D. I can figure out most anything.

13. **Are you comfortable in an unfamiliar situation?**

    __ Yes

    __ No

14. **Your new treat is hidden. How long does it take you to find it?**

    __ A. It's gone get me another one.

    __ B. Run around the room once then bark for more.

    __ C. Sniff it out.

    __ D. Go right to it.

15. **Do you treat your body as a temple, and work hard to improve it?**

    __ Yes

    __ No

16. Celebrity sighting. Lassie is six feet away. Do you...

　　__ A. Sit dumbstruck.

　　__ B. Try to say, "Hhhhi."

　　__ C. Politely ask for a paw print.

　　__ D. Rip the star's collar off and take it home.

17. You just scored a free trip. Are the tickets for...

　　__ A. The Caribbean

　　__ B. London

　　__ C. Vancouver

　　__ D. The Ice Motel

18. Do you have a genius IQ?

　　__ Yes

　　__ No

19. Your perfect summer day includes...

　　__ A. Staying in the air conditioning.

　　__ B. Steak on the porch.

　　__ C. A picnic with the one I love.

　　__ D. I could snooze by the pool all day.

Your total number of A's __ multiplied by 10 = __

                                                +

Your total number of B's __ multiplied by 20 = __

                                                +

Your total number of C's __ multiplied by 30 = __

                                                +

Your total number of D's __ multiplied by 40 = __

                                                +

Your total number of Yes' __ multiplied by 500 = __

                                                =

Total POOCH-ONALITY points _____

Go to **Leader of The Pack** and see what dog breed you are.

I am a _____ dog breed for Pooch-Onality.

Quiz 2: DAPPER DOGS

Answer the following questions, based on height, hair and other physical features, to see what dog breed you most resemble. Add up your points and match it to a breed in **Leader of The Pack**.

A's are worth 10 points.

B's are worth 20 points.

C's are worth 30 points.

D's are worth 40 points.

Yes' are worth 500 points.

No's are worth 0.

1. What height are you?

Short/petite?

__ Yes

__ No

Average height?

　　__ Yes

　　__ No

Tall?

　　__ Yes

　　__ No

Or, are you a giant?

　　__ Yes

　　__ No

2. **Your hair is usually...**

　　__ A. Straight.

　　__ B. Thick and luxurious.

　　__ C. So silky everyone has to touch it.

　　__ D. Coarse.

3. **Which hairstyle works best for you?**

　　__ A. Big hair.

　　__ B. So smooth it should be in commercials.

　　__ C. Shaggy.

　　__ D. Absolutely wash and wear.

What Dog Are You? Discovering Your Inner Pooch

4. **Your eyes are...**

    __ A. Exotic.

    __ B. Oval.

    __ C. Round.

    __ D. Tired.

5. **Choose one body type.**

    Are you an average size?

    __ Yes

    __ No

    Or, a large size?

    __ Yes

    __ No

    Or, an extra large size?

    __ Yes

    __ No

6. **Your facial shape is...**

    __ A. Wedge.

    __ B. Square.

    __ C. Long.

    __ D. Round.

7. Ear size?

    __ A. More on the petite side.

    __ B. Just right.

    __ C. All the better to hear you with, my dear.

    __ D. Can you tie them in a knot? Can you tie them in a bow?

8. Are you a height OTHER THAN short or petite?

    __ Yes

    __ No

9. What's your ear shape?

    __ A. They are small, but angular.

    __ B. Just like everybody else's.

    __ C. Wonderfully rounded, ready for the nibbling.

    __ D. Full lobed.

10. Describe your derrière?

    __ A. Buns of Steel.

    __ B. Perfectly Pert.

    __ C. Royally Rounded.

    __ D. Non-existent.

What Dog Are You? Discovering Your Inner Pooch

11. Mama always said my bones were...

    _ A. Dainty.

    _ B. Small, but tough.

    _ C. Average.

    _ D. Just plain big.

12. Do you have long or medium length hair?

    _ Yes

    _ No

13. Are you taller than the average person?

    _ Yes

    _ No

14. Are you a size OTHER THAN average or small?

    _ Yes

    _ No

15. Your posture is...

    _ A. Slouch.

    _ B. Straight.

    _ C. Throw your chest out and clench your buttocks.

    _ D. Ten-hut! Military stance.

16. **Do you have a massive, giant build?**

  __ Yes

  __ No

17. **If someone described your legs they would say they're...**

  __ A. Stumpy/Sturdy.

  __ B. Short, but shapely.

  __ C. Very well defined.

  __ D. Long, cool drinks of water.

18. **Do you have huge, giant muscles?**

  __ Yes

  __ No

19. **Your feet are?**

  __ A. Boats.

  __ B. Large.

  __ C. Average.

  __ D. Tiny.

What Dog Are You? Discovering Your Inner Pooch

Your total number of A's __ multiplied by 10 = ___

  +

Your total number of B's __ multiplied by 20 = ___

  +

Your total number of C's __ multiplied by 30 = ___

  +

Your total number of D's __ multiplied by 40 = ___

  +

Your total number of Yes' __ multiplied by 500 = ___

  =

Total DAPPER DOGS points _____

Go to **Leader of The Pack** and see what dog breed you are.

I am a _____ dog breed for Dapper Dogs.

QUIZ 3: BISCUITS OR BONES

Keep score and answer the following personal choice questions. Learn which breed may share your same opinions. Total your points then turn to **Leader of The Pack** to see what dog you are.

A's are worth 10 points.

B's are worth 20 points.

C's are worth 30 points.

D's are worth 40 points.

Yes' are worth 500 points.

No's are worth 0.

1. **Your typical day is ...**

    ___ A. Pushing my blanket into the perfect shape.

    ___ B. Give me a new bone and I'm set.

    ___ C. Routine, routine, routine.

    ___ D. Why are there only twenty-four hours in a day?

What Dog Are You? Discovering Your Inner Pooch

2. Does your personal grooming take more than 20 minutes?

    _ Yes

    _ No

3. Which is your favorite sport?

    _ A. Watching a Dog Show on television.

    _ B. Burying a new bone.

    _ C. A long round of fetch.

    _ D. Participating in the Westminster Dog Show.

4. Choose yes to only one of the following statements.

When learning something new...

You go over it several times.

    _ Yes

    _ No

Pick it up easily.

    _ Yes

    _ No

Do as you are instructed.

    _ Yes

    _ No

Forget the lessons, you can teach yourself.

___ Yes

___ No

5. **Ready to play?**

   ___ A. Nah, but I'll watch.

   ___ B. I got the Frisbee.

   ___ C. Grab a few more people, it's GO time.

   ___ D. Call everyone you know. The game is at six.

6. **Do you work out?**

   ___ Yes

   ___ No

7. **Do you show affection?**

   ___ A. No public displays please.

   ___ B. Here, give me your paw.

   ___ C. I hope you like sloppy kisses!

   ___ D. It's nuzzle time.

What Dog Are You? Discovering Your Inner Pooch

8. **Does a day by yourself sound good?**

    __ Yes

    __ No

9. **What's your dream number of pets to live with?**

    __ A. One Neopet/computer pet is fine.

    __ B. Just a couple.

    __ C. An entire herd or flock.

    __ D. A zoo.

10. **You're at a party, do you ...**

    __ A. Fade into the wallpaper.

    __ B. Only talk to other dogs at the water bowl.

    __ C. Tell a few jokes and leave them howling.

    __ D. Clear a table in one swipe, throw a lampshade over your head, and boogie down.

11. **Would you rather go hunting than have a spa day?**

    __ Yes

    __ No

12. When learning a new trick, you think ...

　　__ A. Again? Why?

　　__ B. Tell me just one more time.

　　__ C. Got it!

　　__ D. Don't you have anything harder?

13. If given only two options would you choose to be a guard dog rather than a lapdog?

　　__ Yes

　　__ No

14. How long would it take you to find your hidden bone collection?

　　__ A. Two weeks.

　　__ B. Two days.

　　__ C. Two hours.

　　__ D. Give me a couple of seconds.

15. Could you run the Iditarod?

　　__ Yes

　　__ No

What Dog Are You? Discovering Your Inner Pooch

16. **You're in puppy love. Do you ...**

    __ A. Stare into each other's eyes soulfully?

    __ B. Wag your tail and howl a serenade.

    __ C. Exchange meaningful sniffs.

    __ D. Settle down and have a litter together.

17. **Would you qualify for the K-9 police Unit?**

    __ Yes

    __ No

18. **What do you most like to wear?**

    __ A. Sweater/Sweatshirt.

    __ B. T-shirt.

    __ C. Just a collar.

    __ D. Nothing.

19. **Would you be more likely to enter a bodybuilding contest instead of a kibble-eating contest?**

    __ Yes

    __ No

Lori Lebda & Tami Bergeson

3760-3770 Mastiff	3780 Greater Swiss Mtn Dog
3790-3800 Rottweiler	3810 Bloodhound
3820 Doberman Pinscher	3830-3970 Anatolian Shepherd
3980-4200 Borzoi	4210 Irish Wolfhound
4220 Saint Bernard	4230 Great Pyrenees
4240 Black Russian Terrier	4250 Scottish Deerhound
4260 Bernese Mountain Dog	4270 Alaskan Malamute
4280 Tibetan Mastiff	4290 German Shepherd
4300 Kuvasz	4310 Otter Hound
4320 Komondor	4330+ Newfoundland

TOP DOG

Overall Breed

Let's find out what your Overall breed is! Add together your scores for Pooch-Onality, Dapper Dogs, and Biscuits or Bones, and match that number to one below, and discover your inner dog. Although it is entirely possible to end up being four separate dogs, consider your overall score to be your dominant breed and the other three scores as components of your "puppy genetic makeup." Are you the same as your parents, or were you adopted? What about your friends, are you now siblings?

Total POOCH-ONALITY points _____

+

Total DAPPER DOGS points _____

+

Total BISCUITS OR BONES points _____

=

Overall Dog Score _____

My OVERALL dog breed is a _____.

Lori Lebda & Tami Bergeson

My POOCH-ONALITY dog breed is _____.

My DAPPER DOGS breed is _____.

My BISCIUTS OR BONES dog breed is _____.

1830-2140 Chinese Crested   2150-2200 Chihuahua

2210-2280 Pug   2290-2350 Boston Terrier

2360-2470 Mini Schnauzer   2480-2530 Toy Fox Terrier

2540-2920 Jack Russell   2930-3560 Pekingese

3570 Dandie Dinmont Terrier   3580-3630 Australian Terrier

3640-3670 Lhasa Apso   3680-3700 Bedlington Terrier

3710-3730 Silky Terrier   3740-3760 Yorkshire Terrier

3770-3790 Pomeranian   3800-3820 Shih Tzu

3830-3850 Maltese   3860-3880 Brussels Griffon

3890-3910 Tibetan Spaniel   1920-3940 Bichon Frise

3950-3970 Bolognese   3980-4000 Japanese Chin

4010-4030 Affenpinscher   4040-4060 Papillon

4070-4100 Havanese   4110-4420 Coton De Tulear

What Dog Are You? Discovering Your Inner Pooch

4430-5130 Chinese Shar-Pei	5140-5170 Dachshund
5180-5230 Aust Cattle Dog	5240-5260 Australian Shepherd
5270-5290 Card Welsh Corgi	5300-5320 Brittany
5330-5350 American Bulldog	5360-5410 Basenji
5420-5470 Dingo	5480-5510 Cocker Spaniel
5520-5910 Beagle	5920-6600 Toy Am Eskimo
6610-6630 Shetland Sheepdog	6640-6670 Puli
6680-6700 Bearded Collie	6710-6750 Shiba Inu
6760-6790 Siberian Husky	6800-6850 Tibetan Terrier
6860-6900 Port Water Dog	6910 Polish Lowland Sheepdog
6920-6950 Eng Springer Spnl	6960-6980 Poodle
6990-7030 Am Water Spaniel	7040-7420 Dalmatian
7430-8200 Chesapeake Bay Rtvr	8210-8230 Greyhound
8240-8260 Curly-Coated Rtvr	8270-8300 Am Staff Terrier
8310-8330 German S/H Pointer	8340-8360 Boxer
8370-8390 Vizla	8400-8440 Basset Hound

8450-8470	Pharaoh Hound	8480-8500	Belgian Malinois
8510-8530	Labrador Retriever	8540-8570	Ibizan Hound
8580	Rhodesian Ridgeback	8590-8620	Redbone Coonhound
8630-8650	Coonhound B & T	8660-8680	Plott
8690-8920	English Foxhound	8930-9580	Chow Chow
9590-9700	Clumber Spaniel	9710-9730	Samoyed
9740-9760	Collie	9770-9790	Afghan Hound
9800-9820	Golden Retriever	9830-9850	Norwegian Elkhound
9860-9880	American Foxhound	9890-9940	Irish Setter
9950-10420	Saluki	10430-11190	Great Dane
11200-11230	Akita	11240-11260	Dogo Argentino
11270-11290	Mastiff	11300-11350	Gtr Swiss MtnDog
11360-11400	Rottweiler	11410-11440	Bloodhound
11450-11470	Doberman Pin	11480-11920	Anatolian Shep
11930-12600	Borzoi	12610-12640	Irish Wolfhound
12650-12670	Saint Bernard	12680-12700	Great Pyrenees

What Dog Are You? Discovering Your Inner Pooch

12710-12730 Blk Russian Terr   12740-12760 Scot Deerhound

12770-12790 Bernese Mtn. Dog   12800-12830 Alaskan Malamute

12840-12850 Tibetan Mastiff   12860-12880 German Shepherd

12890-12910 Kuvasz   12920-12940 Otter Hound

12950-12970 Komondor   12980-13320 Newfoundland

THE KENNEL

Who's In Your Pack

Ever wonder why you just clicked with a new friend right off the bat? Have you wanted to try a new restaurant, but your best bud wants to stick with the same old one? Do you ever wonder why a friend acts the way they do? Learn more about your family, friends and your own dog personality by understanding dog groups and characteristics.

Can you identify each of your family and friends in the dog personalities? In their own unique way all dogs compliment each other and help to keep a balanced way of life.

After you have taken the three quizzes use your overall dog breed, and find out which dog group you, and your family and friends are in.

Gems:
Affenpinscher, Brussels Griffon, Chihuahua, Chinese Crested, Havanese, Japanese Chin, Maltese, Papillon, Pekingese, Pomeranian, Pug, Shih Tzu, Silky Terrier, Toy American Eskimo, Toy Fox Terrier, Yorkshire Terrier.

Trend Setters:
Bichon Frise, Bolognese, Boston Terrier, Chinese Shar-Pei, Chow Chow, Coton De Tulear, Dalmatian, Dingo, Lhasa Apso, Poodle, Tibetan Spaniel, Tibetan Terrier, Shiba Inu.

Feisty Friends:
American Staffordshire Terrier, Australian Terrier, Bedlington Terrier, Dandie Dinmont Terrier, Jack Russell, Mini Schnauzer.

Private Eyes:
Afghan Hound, American Foxhound, Basenji, Basset Hound, Beagle, Bloodhound, Borzoi, Coonhound B & T, Dachshund, English Foxhound, Greyhound, Ibizan Hound, Irish Wolfhound, Norwegian Elkhound, Otter Hound, Pharaoh Hound, Plott, Redbone Coonhound, Rhodesian Ridgeback, Scottish Deerhound, Saluki.

Guardians:
Akita, Alaskan Malamute, American Bulldog, Anatolian Shepherd, Black Russian Terrier, Boxer, Bernese Mountain Dog, Doberman Pinscher, Dogo Argentino, Great Dane, Great Pyrenees, Greater Swiss Mountain Dog, Komondor, Kuvasz, Mastiff, Newfoundland, Portuguese Water Dog, Rottweiler, Saint Bernard, Samoyed, Siberian Husky, Tibetan Mastiff.

Contenders:
American Water Spaniel, Brittany, Chesapeake Bay Retriever, Clumber Spaniel, Cocker Spaniel, Curly-Coated Retriever, English Springer Spaniel, German Shorthaired Pointer, Golden Retriever, Irish Setter, Labrador Retriever, Vizla.

The Alphas:
Australian Cattle Dog, Australian Shepherd, Bearded Collie, Belgian Malinois, Cardigan Welsh Corgi, Collie, German Shepherd, Polish Lowland Sheepdog, Puli, Shetland Sheepdog.

Gems:
If you're honest I'm sure you'll even admit that on occasion a muzzle might have come in handy! Good or bad Gems never have a problem letting you know what's on their mind. You're

always enjoyable... even sarcasm is barked in a pleasant tone. The worst situation for you is to be chained to a stake, socially isolated, and all alone.

You tend to like the trendy, diamond studded collars in life and don't mind shelling out the biscuits to buy them. You're not a show off though, and gladly let your friends play with your new toys. Always friendly, you're the first to show appreciation and nuzzle your friends and family.

After a hard days work, you can be very rambunctious and silly, almost to the extreme. You might even be willing to call in sick at work just to keep a party going. A Gems idea of enjoying life is to have every waking moment spent and cherished with family and friends. Even when you're taking a vacation the destination would be of no consequence, as long as your circle of friends and family were there.

Gems can be picked out of a crowd by their relaxed and fun nature, and would gladly meet your gaze with a smile. You might be an entrepreneur, a member of the local drama club or do volunteer work. Gems are most compatible with the Trend Setters and the Feisty Friends, but will trade barks with the Alphas. Celebrities that may be in this group are: Dolly Parton, Dakota Fanning, Jennifer Love-Hewitt, Michael J. Fox, Elijah Wood and Johnny Depp.

Trend Setters:
Trend Setter dogs are a happy-go-lucky bunch. You have no trouble yapping be it in a pack of people or one on one with your best buds. Knowing a little bit about almost everything you can carry on a conversation in a wide array of topics. While you don't mind a spirited debate, you're alone or quiet time is also important to you.

When making those big purchases you're more likely to think about it for a while, and look at all the squeaky toys and bones available. In fact you might even end up chasing your tail while you decide. Your tastes vary and can be hard to pin down.

You have a great sense of humor and are fun-loving, but know not to go overboard with silliness. Trend Setter dogs like things on a short leash, no extremes. Living life to the fullest would include experiencing different cultures and life from different points of view. A good vacation would be a balance of relaxation and excitement.

Trend Setter dogs can be picked out of a crowd by their distinctive appearance, carefree laugh and ability to greet people with a friendly sniff or paw on the back. You might be a member of the local 4-H club, 24-hour gym, or enrolled in a fashion, art or drama class. Trend Setters are most compatible with the Feisty Friends and the Contenders, but will trade barks with the Private Eyes. Celebrities that may be in this group are: Angelina Jolie, Clay Aiken, Cher, Hugh Jackman, Hilary Duff and Will Smith.

Feisty Friends:

Feisty Friends are happy, scrappy and determined, almost to the point of being stubborn. Your circle of friends usually includes someone with just as feisty a personality as yours to keep up with you, someone to be the peacemaker, and a few "yes dogs," just for fun.

When it comes to buying a ritzy doghouse or trendy leash there will be no waiting for birthdays or holidays, you just go and get it. You may be a bit boastful, but you don't care what others think. To you most everything is just a matter of fact, that's the way it is, and there is not much room for change.

Feisty Friends enjoy every minute of every day, and don't plan on ever missing out on anything. No chain wanted here, you have boundless energy and drive. A perfect weekend or vacation would be a destination of endless fun at a theme park, a mega mall or maybe even playing the Wii.

In a crowd, Feisty Friends would be the ones mingling to talk to everyone. You might be a member of a debate team, a stand-up comedian or on a rowing team. Feisty Friends are most compatible with the Gems and the Contenders, but will trade barks with the Alphas. Celebrities that may be in this group are: Lindsay Lohan, Robin Williams, Kelly Rippa, Ben Stiller, Kathy Griffin and Jack Black.

Private Eyes:
Private Eyes have exceptional communication skills, especially when yapping about a topic of interest. You're not big on small talk, and have no problem abruptly butting into another conversation and leaving. Luckily, your few long-standing friends understand you well enough not to be offended. If your friends were asked to describe you in one word it would be consistent.

Having the latest treats and collars is not important to you. The same old ones work just fine. Private Eyes have a tendency to get tunnel vision. When working on a new project, you are completely consumed by it and follow through from start to finish, making it top priority with no exceptions.

You live by the motto work hard and play harder. You might become too careless or too carefree. Know your boundaries and stay within them. Your weekends or vacations need to be structured with little to no down time.

Private Eyes could be picked out of a crowd by their constant scanning of the masses and alert manner. You might be a member of the school newspaper staff, an environmental activist or active in extreme sports. Private Eyes are most compatible with Alphas and Contenders, but will trade barks with Guardians. Celebrities that may be in this group are: Tony Hawk, Courtney Love, Charlie Sheen, Whitney Houston, Dennis Rodman and Rosie O'Donnell.

Guardians:
Guardian dogs are friendly and open with companions. Your circle of friends and family may be small, but is unrivaled by your quiet, intense loyalty and love. Due to your strong family bonds, you are always considerate, kind and ready to lend a helpful paw.

When it comes to money, you live in a modest doghouse, but do have a few high priced chew toys to keep up with your daring side. A few of your extra curricular activities help keep you fit and active, and require strength or endurance. You're willing to try anything at least once.

Adventurous by nature, it's always fun to be around you. You're responsible and mature with a very appealing dry wit.

You live life to its fullest, and would rather experience things than read about them. An ideal weekend or vacation would be a chance to do something you have never done before.

Guardian dogs can be picked out of a crowd by their quiet demeanor, keen listening skills and watchful eyes. You might be a member of a Volunteer Fire Department, ROTC or an honors program. Guardian dogs are most compatible with the Trend Setters and the Private Eyes, but will trade barks with Feisty Friends. Celebrities that may be in this group are: Clint Eastwood, Jennifer Garner, Dwayne "The Rock" Johnson, Geena Davis, Michael Jordan, Katie Couric.

Contenders:

Contenders are yappy, and have a well-rounded, cooperative personality. You don't need a large pack of friends, but cherish your few long-standing ones. You are able to understand and learn new things fast, and able to make quick decisions based on pure instinct.

You like your digs comfortable, and have a real thirst for the latest high tech toys. You try and keep pace with the people and environment around you. At work and at home you give one hundred and ten percent, and wouldn't want it any other way.

If your down time is not structured you have a tendency to endlessly play fetch. Plan ahead, but don't end up stuck in the doghouse. Not wanting to miss any opportunity to live life to the fullest, you are always active and on the go. A perfect weekend or vacation would be to a tropical all-inclusive resort.

Contenders can be spotted in a crowd by their fast tapping feet, high bouncing knees and constant checking for the time. You might be a member of any varsity sport, a mentor or a diplomat. Contenders are most compatible with the Guardians and the Alphas, but will trade barks with the Trend Setters. Celebrities that may be in this group with you are: Michael Phelps, Michele Kwan, Howie Long, Serena Williams, Jim Carey and Cameron Diaz.

Alpha Dogs:

With all your managerial experience woofing commands

is not a problem for you. When it comes to personal matters, you may confide in only a handful of friends or family. Alpha dogs don't need a large pack of friends, and prefer the company of only a select few. Due to your large, bounding personality, people naturally gravitate toward you.

Alpha dogs prefer everything to be in balance, and skip the extras. You always have appropriate attire for each occasion, and look regal and elegant. Your warm, friendly disposition invites people to ask for advice or help. You have well-honed intuition, and have the ability to handle any given situation.

You may feel that even down time or a vacation can be put to productive use. A possible adventure for you would be to learn a new language. Alpha dogs can be picked out of a crowd by their commanding presence and friendly manner. You might be a member of the student council, a team-leader or create a new charity. Alpha dogs are most compatible with the Guardians and the Private Eyes, but will trade barks with the Gems. Celebrities that may be in this group with you are: Oprah Winfrey, Alan Alda, Hillary Rodham Clinton, Mel Gibson, Bill Gates and Donald Trump.

PUPPY LOVE

What's Your Sign

ARIES: March 21 - April 19
You are a fiercely loyal, loving and generous friend and family member. Courage and bravery are inherent, especially when facing an enormous problem or opponent. Backing down is never an option. You will be the first one to jump up and help a friend.

Occasionally that same good willed enthusiasm has you running in circles. Keep busy, and redirect any worries in a new direction. Try breaking in that new frisbee or chew toy.

You need new challenges and variety in your daily life, and prefer to direct others rather than they direct you. A good career choice may be in journalism, engineering, doctor, explorer, radio and TV, or any type of leadership role.

Aries get along best with Leo and Sagittarius then Gemini, Libra and Aquarius. Signs that make your fur stand on end are Taurus, Scorpio, Virgo, Pisces and Capricorn. You may be ready to take a bite out of Cancer.

Your best day in a week is Tuesday, your true color is red and your lucky numbers are one and nine. Other Arians are: Aretha Franklin, Dennis Quaid, Ashley Judd, Quentin Tarantino, Justice Sandra Day O'Connor, Tommy Hilfiger.

TAURUS: April 20 - May 20
You are the reliable, consistent one in the bunch. Always kind and thoughtful, you are a warmhearted friend and family member. A lot of your daily decisions are based on emotion and feeling,

rather than what your head is telling you. Being consistent is a great asset, but if taken to the extreme your friends may decide you can't learn new tricks. Try to be a little flexible now and then.

Taureans are naturally artistic, motivated and thorough. You will do well as a builder, banker, real estate broker, teacher, singer or craftsmen.

Taurus get along best with Virgo and Capricorn then Cancer, Pisces and, Scorpio. Signs that make your fur stand on end are Aries, Libra, Gemini, Sagittarius and Aquarius. You may be ready to take a bite out of the Leos.

Your best day of the week is Friday, your color is light blue and pink, and your lucky numbers are four and six. Other Taureans are: Uma Thurman, Tony Danza, Renee Zellwegger, George Lucas, Carol Burnett, William Shakespeare.

GEMINI: May 21 - June 21

You're always ready to grab the leash and go, be it rolling around the backyard or playing catch on the beach. Gemini's boundless energy and youthful zest for life is contagious. It's no wonder others are naturally drawn to you.

While enthusiasm is great, don't let it lead your life. Make decisions based on logic not on what seems like a good idea at the time. Think things through and be consistent with your choices.

You are a free spirit that takes multitasking to a new level. A good career choice would be a diplomat, instructor, publicist, writer or lawyer.

A Gemini will get along best with a Libra and Aquarius then Aries, Sagittarius and Leo. Signs that make your fur stand on end are Cancer, Scorpio, Taurus and Pisces. You may be ready to take a bite out of the Virgos.

Your best day of the week is Wednesday, your color is yellow and your lucky numbers are five and nine. Other Gemini are: Angelina Jolie, Johnny Depp, Paula Abdul, George Washington, Venus Williams, Bob Dylan.

CANCER: June 22 - July 22

Being a Cancer you are very in tune with other people's

emotion. You are very intuitive and sympathetic with friends and family. Your imagination never ceases to amaze everyone.

While it's great to be a lap dog, don't forget to find your buried toys in the backyard every once in a while. You are known to get over emotional and moody in tense, personal situations. It would hurt you deeply to be thought of as interfering or clingy.

Due to your interest and compassion in other people a good job choice might be anything in the public sector, medical field, a politician, musician or maybe even a chef.

Cancer will get along best with a Scorpio and Pisces then Taurus, Capricorn and Virgo. Signs that make your fur stand on end are Aquarius, Leo, Gemini and Sagittarius. You may be ready to take a bite out of the Libras.

Your best day of the week is Monday, your colors are sea green and silver, and your lucky numbers are three and seven. Other Cancerians are: Pamela Anderson, Tom Cruise, Helen Keller, Matthew Fox, Ann Landers, Jimmy Smits.

LEO: July 23 - August 22

Your passion and creative ways rule you. Everything is done with great intensity. You're generous and wholehearted with everything in your life. When you're friends with someone you are best friends forever. Watch your enthusiasm and use self-control. It's easy to take the simplest situation and go overboard seeming bossy or superior. Your friends think you're tops, but there's no need to flaunt it.

Leos are creative, ambitious and natural leaders. You will do best as a President, Chairman or on a Board of Directors. Another good choice is a stage or film star, musician, singer, manager or organizer.

Leos will get along best with an Aries and Sagittarius then Gemini, Aquarius and Libra. Signs that make your fur stand on end are Capricorn, Cancer, Virgo, Taurus and Pisces. You may be ready to take a bite out of a Scorpio.

Your best day of the week is Sunday. Your color is orange and gold. Your lucky numbers are eight and nine. Other Leos are: Robert De Niro, Neil Armstrong, Melanie Griffith, Antonio Banderas, Hilary Swank, Alfred Hitchcock.

VIRGO: August 23 - September 22
You may be shy, but you are very reliable, serene and intelligent. You're quiet manner disguises your playful, silly side. You are a true friend through thick and thin.

Try to loosen up and not be ruled by the kennel's ridged schedule. Being conservative has its rewards, but sometimes you need to relax and try something unplanned or out of the ordinary. Just take a deep breathe and go for it!

Virgos are all about the details. You're practical and logic rules your decision-making. Good career choices may be a teacher, technician, psychologist, historian, researcher, programmer, and statistician.

Virgos will get along best with a Taurus and Capricorn then Cancer, Pisces and Scorpio. Signs that make your fur stand on end are Libra, Aries, Aquarius, Leo and Gemini. You may be ready to take a bite out of Sagittarius.

Your best day of the week is Wednesday. Your color is navy blue and gray. Your lucky numbers are three and five. Other Virgos are: Cameron Diaz, Adam Sandler, Jane Curtin, Sean Connery, LeAnn Rimes, Harry Connick, Jr.

LIBRA: September 23 - October 22
Libras know how to sit, lay-down, roll over and will even play dead for that extra biscuit. You don't mind sitting still for the long grooming sessions, and always look elegant. You're sociable demeanor is loveable, and wins everyone over.

We all know you're charming, but find your boundaries, when enough is enough stop. You don't want to look self-indulgent. Sometimes too many options can cause indecision. Learn to trust your first instinct and stick to it.

Libras are naturally trustworthy and creative. A possible career choice may include an administrator, finance, designer, law, civil servant, diplomat, humanitarian or entertainer.

Libras will get along best with a Gemini, Aquarius, Leo,

Aries and Sagittarius. Signs that make your fur stand on end are Taurus, Scorpio, Virgo, Pisces and Cancer. You may be ready to take a bite out of Capricorn.

Your best day of the week is Friday, your color is blue and lavender, and your lucky numbers are six and nine. Other Libras are: Heather Locklear, Will Smith, Barbara Walters, John Melloncamp, Susan Sarandon, Johnny Carson.

SCORPIO: October 23 - November 21

There's never a dull day with a Scorpio. Your energy and passion for life is electric. You are intensely loyal, and would lay down your life without a second thought to protect a loved one.

While your determination is admirable, don't get carried away. If taken too far it can be seen as stubbornness. Set boundaries so you don't get obsessive.

A Scorpio's inner intensity and curious nature makes them well adept for a career in psychology, research, detective, law, military, surgeon, or scientist.

Scorpios will get along best with a Cancer and Pisces then Virgo, Taurus and Capricorn. Signs that make your fur stand on end are Aries, Libra, Gemini, Sagittarius and Leo. You may be ready to take a bite out of Aquarians.

Your best day of the week is Tuesday, your color is deep red and your lucky numbers are two and four. Other Scorpios are: Julia Roberts, Sean Combs Demi Moore, Dylan McDermott, Hillary Rodham Clinton, Pablo Picasso.

SAGITTARIUS: November 22 - December 21

Your good-natured, optimistic take on life is refreshing. You are rambunctious, and love to mix it up a bit, and if you cause a little fun turmoil along the way that's okay!

Keep your adventurous side realistic. Without clear boundaries you may become reckless or irresponsible. Even when you think you know every possible scenario in a situation take the time to listen to a new perspective, don't be stubborn and say no.

Your adaptable nature opens a wide range of career possibilities including a musician, philosopher, scientist, law, politics, public service, travel agent, pilot, athlete, or bookkeeper.

Sagittarians will get along best with a Leo and Aries then Libra, Gemini and Aquarius. Signs that make your fur stand on end are Capricorn, Cancer, Scorpio, Taurus and Virgo. You may be ready to take a bite out of Pisces.

Your best day of the week is Thursday, your color is purple, and your lucky numbers are five and seven. Other Sagittarians are: Teri Hatcher, Steven Spielberg, Jane Austen, Mark Twain, Tina Turner, Kiefer Sutherland.

CAPRICORN: December 22 - January 19

You prefer the term sensible, so what if you evaluate five different squeaky toys before choosing one? You'll be happy with your choice having thought it through. Patience and practicality suit you well.

On the other paw, some might accuse you of being stingy and unable to make a decision, of course this was right after you comparison shopped at eight stores then went home with no toys. Live a little, and expand your perimeter of what's acceptable. Change is good.

Count on a Capricorn to see the big picture. Good career choices may be accountant, lawyer, doctor, public servant, teacher, engineer, farmer, conductor or manager.

Capricorns will get along best with a Virgo and Taurus then Scorpio, Cancer and Pisces. Signs that make your fur stand on end are Aquarius, Leo, Gemini, Sagittarius and Libra. You may be ready to take a bite out of Aries.

Your best day of the week is Saturday, your color is dark green and brown, and your lucky numbers are two and eight. Other Capricorns are: Patrick Dempsey, Nicholas Cage, Diane Keaton, Orlando Bloom, Annie Lennox, Denzel Washington.

AQUARIUS: January 20 - February 18

You're a loyal friend and always willing to listen closely. When you're bored you have an uncanny knack of turning almost any household item into a toy, and play with it all day.

What Dog Are You? Discovering Your Inner Pooch

You can be a bit of a daredevil, and have been known to get extreme with some of your antics. It's always your unpredictable side that gets you into trouble. When this happens it's easy to understand why your friends might distance themselves.

Aquarians do best with a clear agenda, and excel when working in groups. A good career choice may be as a staff photographer, historian, researcher, computer technologist, scientist, writer, teacher, welfare worker, or in the entertainment field.

Aquarians get along best with a Libra and Gemini then Sagittarius, Leo and Aries. Signs that make your fur stand on end are Capricorn, Cancer, Virgo, Pisces and Scorpio. You may be ready to take a bite out of Taurus.

Your best day of the week is Wednesday, your color is electric blue and your lucky numbers are one and seven. Other Aquarians are: Ellen DeGeneres, Charles Darwin, Sheryl Crow, Eddie Van Halen, John Travolta, Norman Rockwell.

PISCES: February 19 - March 20
Always charming, Pisces are adaptable to most situations, and like variety and a little mystery in the day. You thrive on new projects and adventures, and can easily go overboard with gusto.

Playtime is great, but make no mistake that when you're done playing- you're done, your alone time is just as important. You seem to march to your own drum, and have trouble following a routine or schedule.

Pisces are very intuitive and insightful. In a career you need the room to make most of the choices on your own. You would make an excellent nurse, veterinarian, law enforcement, civil service, chef, astronomer, or in the entertainment field.

Pisces will get along best with a Scorpio and Cancer then Capricorn, Virgo and Taurus. Signs that make your fur stand on end are Libra, Aries, Aquarius, Leo and Sagittarius. You may be ready to take a bite out of Gemini.

Your best day of the week is Friday, your color is pale green and turquoise, and your lucky numbers are two and six. Other Pisces are: Drew Barrymore, Billy Crystal, Cindy Crawford, Albert Einstein, Queen Latifah, Kurt Russell.

Ca-NINE

How Old Are You

It was once believed that one human year is equal to seven dog years, however that is not very accurate since dogs reach adulthood within the first couple of years, instead of later in life like humans. It is now estimated that the human equivalent of a 1-year-old dog is just over ten years (for the first 2 years of life), after that each year is equivalent to about four human years.

Human Years = Dog Years

1 yr = 6 wk	2 yr = 2 mo 3 wk	3 yr = 4 mo
4 yr = 5 mo 1 wk	5 yr = 6 mo	6 yr = 7 mo
7 yr = 8 mo	8 yr = 9 mo	9 yr = 10 mo
10 yr = 11 mo	11 yr = 1 yr	12 yr = 1 yr 1½ mo
13 yr = 1 yr 3 mo	14 yr = 4 mo	15 yr = 1 yr 5 mo
16 yr = 1 yr 6½ mo	17 yr = 1 yr 7¾ mo	18 yr = 1yr 9 mo
19 yr = 1 yr 10 mo	20 yr = 1 yr 11 mo	21 yr = 2 yr
22 yr = 2 yr 3 mo	23 yr = 2 yr 6 mo	24 yr = 2 yr 9 mo

What Dog Are You? Discovering Your Inner Pooch

Human Years = Dog Years

25 yr = 3 yr	26 yr = 3 yr 3 mo	27 yr = 3 yr 6 mo
28 yr = 3 yr 9 mo	29 yr = 4 yr	30 yr = 4 yr 3 mo
31 yr = 4 yr 6 mo	32 yr = 4 yr 9 mo	33 yr = 5 yr
34 yr = 5 yr 3 mo	35 yr = 5 yr 6 mo	36 yr = 5 yr 9 mo
37 yr = 6 yr	38 yr = 6 yr 3 mo	39 yr = 6 yr 6 mo
40 yr = 6 yr 9 mo	41 yr = 7 yr	42 yr = 7 yr 3 mo
43 yr = 7 yr 6 mo	44 yr = 7 yr 9 mo	45 yr = 8 yr
46 yr = 8 yr 3 mo	47 yr = 8 yr 6 mo	48 yr = 8 yr 9 mo
49 yr = 9 yr	50 yr = 9 yr 3 mo	51 yr = 9 yr 6 mo
52 yr = 9 yr 9 mo	53 yr = 10 yr	54 yr = 10 yr 3 mo
55 yr = 10 yr 6 mo	56 yr = 10 yr 9 mo	57 yr = 11 yr
58 yr = 11 yr 3 mo	59 yr = 11 yr 6 mo	60 yr = 11 yr 9 mo
61 yr = 12 yr	62 yr = 12 yr 3 mo	63 yr = 12 yr 6 mo
64 yr = 12 yr 9 mo	65 yr = 13 yr	66 yr = 13 yr 3 mo
67 yr = 13 yr 6 mo	68 yr = 13 yr 9 mo	69 yr = 14 yr
70 yr = 14 yr 3 mo	71 yr = 14 yr 6 mo	72 yr = 14 yr 9 mo

Lori Lebda & Tami Bergeson

Human Years = Dog Years

73 yr = 15 yr	74 yr = 15 yr 3 mo	75 yr = 15 yr 6 mo
76 yr = 15 yr 9 mo	77 yr = 16 yr	78 yr = 16 yr 3 mo
79 yr = 16 yr 6 mo	80 yr = 16 yr 9 mo	81 yr = 17 yr
82 yr = 17 yr 3 mo	83 yr = 17 yr 6 mo	84 yr = 17 yr 9 mo
85 yr = 18 yr	86 yr = 18 yr 3 mo	87 yr = 18 yr 6 mo
88 yr = 18 yr 9 mo	89 yr = 19 yr	90 yr = 19 yr 3 mo
91 yr = 19 yr 6 mo	92 yr = 19 yr 9 mo	93 yr = 20 yr
94 yr = 20 yr 3 mo	95 yr = 20 yr 6 mo	96 yr = 20 yr 9 mo
97 yr = 21 yr	98 yr = 21 yr 3 mo	99 yr = 21 yr 6 mo
100 yr = 21 yr 9 mo		

PUREBRED PICTURES

Find your Photo

You will find 100 dogs playing on the next 10 pages. Wondering what the number is for? Match it to a number in **100 Breeds: Dog Summaries** to learn about your new self!

Lori Lebda & Tami Bergeson

What Dog Are You? Discovering Your Inner Pooch

What Dog Are You? Discovering Your Inner Pooch

Lori Lebda & Tami Bergeson

What Dog Are You? Discovering Your Inner Pooch

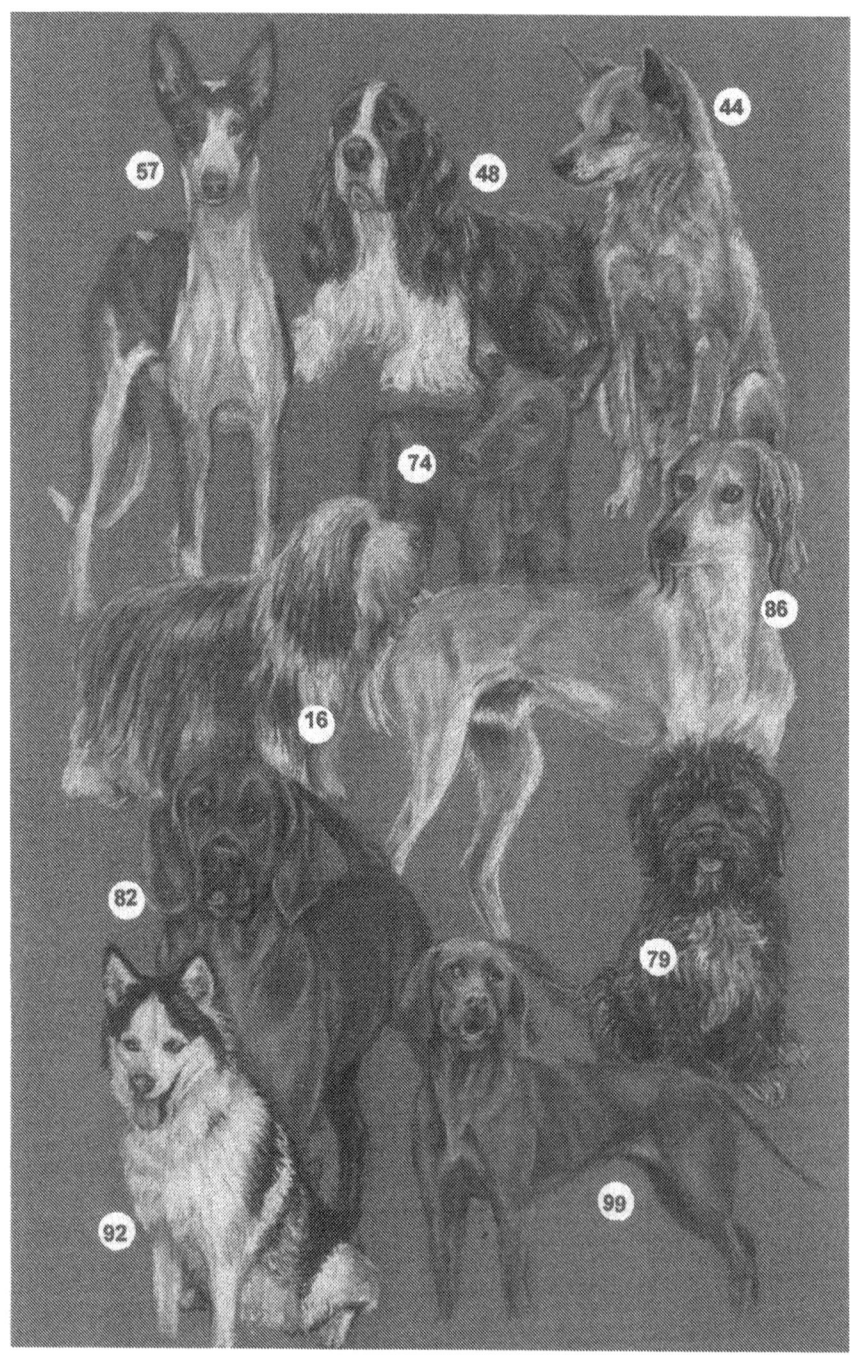

Lori Lebda & Tami Bergeson

What Dog Are You? Discovering Your Inner Pooch

Lori Lebda & Tami Bergeson

What Dog Are You? Discovering Your Inner Pooch

100 DOGS

Breed Summaries

Each dog group is different with each having a special attribute. The main groups are the Toy dogs, Non-Sporting, Terriers, Sporting, Hounds, Working or Herding dogs. Most of the Toys were developed to be miniature versions of our most beloved pooches. The Non-Sporting group consists mainly of dogs that do not fit into any other category, but are unique none the less. The Terriers are a scrappy bunch originally used to kill vermin, but mostly now used as companions. The Sporting group accompanies the hunter, and points the prey out, gets the prey moving or after its shot, they retrieve it. The Hound group also tracks quarry, but many times will do it separately from its owner. They have exceptional sight or scent abilities. The Working group use their brawn and bravery for protecting or rescuing humans. Lastly, the Herding group lives to control the movements of other animals, and is able to accept commands from an owner and work independently.

The one hundred dogs used in this book are listed alphabetically and numerically (for their pictures).

1. Affenpinscher
The Monkey Dog. This breed is one of the oldest terriers, and was developed in Germany. They were used to hunt vermin, but now are mostly companions. They are playful and loyal.

2. Afghan Hound
The Regal Hound. The Afghan has an air of elegance and

glamour. They can cross great distances in adverse terrains while chasing game. The Afghan hound is graceful and agile.

3. Akita
The National Treasure of Japan. Akitas are heavy boned dogs that have webbed feet for swimming. They don't bark often so when they do regard it as a warning bark. Akita's have a fierce love and loyalty to family members.

4. Alaskan Malamute
The Inuit Dog. Inuit tribes used these dogs to pull heavy weight as sled dogs over long distance in the harsh Alaskan climate. They are cherished and dignified dogs.

5. American Bulldog
The Wrangler. This breed was used to wrangle cattle on the early frontier. They are strong enough to hold back cattle, and avoid hooves at the same time. They are friendly and clever.

6. American Foxhound
The Fastest Foxhound. The American Foxhound is exceptional in hunting, tracking and agility, and makes a good watchdog. They can chase foxes in packs and can run for hours. They are bright, active, brave and friendly dogs.

7. American Staffordshire Terrier
The Ultimate Fighting Machine. This dog was originally bred for fighting, but is now used for protection. One of the famous Staffs was Pete the Pup, Dog Star of the original Our Gang comedies of the 1930's. They are quick, strong guard dogs.

8. American Water Spaniel
The Skiff Dog. The American Water Spaniel was developed as a hunting dog able to fit in and retrieve from canoes or skiffs. Their unique coat is water resistant. They are active and smart.

9. Anatolian Shepherd
World's Best Guard Dog. Anatolian Shepherds accompanied nomadic Turkish shepherds and helped to protect their flocks. They are rugged, powerful and able to withstand harsh climates. This breed is courageous, smart and devoted.

10. Australian Cattle Dog
The Heeler. Australian Cattle dogs were bred to heel and bite cattle in the rugged Australian Outback. This breed is better as a one-person dog. They are always alert and trustworthy.

11. Australian Shepherd
Best Friend. Australian Shepherds have strong herding and sheep guarding instincts. Reserved with strangers this Aussie is dependable and devoted to their family.

12. Australian Terrier
The Spirited Aussie. Decades ago this breed was created by crossing many different breeds of terriers. They have watchdog and ratting abilities. They are fearless and faithful.

13. Basenji
The Congo Dog. In the 1930's the Basenji was brought to Europe from the forests of Africa. Basenjis wash themselves like a cat. They are elegant, energetic and friendly.

14. Basset Hound
The Hush Puppy. The Basset Hound originated in France, and the word "Basset" means "low set" in French. They have a keen sense of smell and can cover great distances in a short time. Basset Hounds are loving and gentle.

15. Beagle
Joe Cool. Developed in England, these small, scent hounds were originally used to hunt rabbits. For over fifty years the Beagle has ranked in the top 10 most loved breeds in the USA. They are devoted, trusted and loveable.

16. Bearded Collie
Long Beard. This breed was developed in Scotland, and used for herding. The hair under their chin is unusually long, and gives the impression of a beard. They're happy and kind dogs.

17. Bedlington Terrier
The Sheep Dog. Bedlingtons have an unusual soft, wooly, curly-coat. Originally bred to hunt vermin and small game, today they are used as watchdogs. They are quiet and gentle.

18. Belgian Malinois
The Guardian. This breed almost became extinct during World War II. They are natural guardians, protectors and rescue dogs. Belgian Malinois are reliable and confident.

19. Bernese Mountain Dog
The Mountain Dog. In ancient Rome, this breed was used as sentries for the Roman army when they marched through the Swiss Alps. They are kind, trustworthy and protective.

20. Bichon Frise
Happy Go Lucky. This all white fluff ball has a double coat of loose curls. They travel well and long ago were used as an item of barter for sailors. They are smart, lively and happy.

21. Black Russian Terrier
The Russian Soldier. The Russian army used the Black Russian Terrier extensively. Their thick, black coat can withstand cold winters. They are strong, proud and faithful.

22. Bloodhound
The Warrior Hound. Bloodhounds are believed to be descendants from William the Conqueror's dogs, and were given as gifts to royalty. They have a keen scent ability, superior to other hounds, and are powerful, yet graceful.

23. Bolognese
The Renaissance Dog. Originated from the Mediterranean, the Bolo was given as royal gifts. They have been depicted in Renaissance art and writings. They are smart and happy dogs.

24. Boston Terrier
Pure USA. The Boston Terrier is one of the few breeds to be made in American. They were originally called a Boston Bull. They are very gentle, protective and bright dogs.

25. Borzoi
The Graceful Giant. The Borzoi is also known as the Russian Wolfhound. They were bred for beauty, elegance and speed. These dogs are very quiet and rarely bark.

26. Boxer
The Patrol Dog. Boxers are one of the first breeds in Germany to be trained as police dogs. They combine strength and agility with elegance and style. Boxers are playful and patient.

27. Brittany
The Bird Dog. The Brittany's first love is birds then people. They make an excellent hunting dog, and are the only spaniel that point to game. They are good with children and energetic.

28. Brussels Griffon
Mr./Mrs. Personality. The Brussels Griffon originated in Brussels, Belgium. Their face is unique and has a human facial expression to it. They are good-natured and happy.

29. Cardigan Welsh Corgi
The Dynamo. This breed originated in the remote hills of Cardiganshire, Wales, and was used for farm help, guard dogs and companions. They are fast, friendly and loyal.

30. Chesapeake Bay Retriever
The Swimmer. Named for the Chesapeake Bay in Maryland,

these webbed foot dogs love the water. They can retrieve a duck or even a drowning child. Chessies are bright and happy.

31. Chihuahua
The Taco Bell Dog. Chihuahuas are named after the Mexican city they were found in. Their exact origin is disputed and thought to include China or Egypt. They are playful and loyal.

32. Chinese Crested
The Powder Puff. This breed only has a small tuft of hair on the head, feet and tail. They are believed to have originated in Africa then developed in China. They are smart and elegant.

33. Chinese Shar-Pei
The Primordial One. This ancient breed is thought to have originated in a small village of Tai Li in Kwangtung Province, China. They have loose skin that gives it a wrinkled look. They are regal and love their family.

34. Chow Chow
The Lion Dog. This Chinese breed dates back to the Han Dynasty about 150 B.C. They have a blue and black colored tongue. They are proud and well mannered.

35. Clumber Spaniel
The Noble Frenchman. The Clumber was developed in the late 1700's France, and was then taken to Clumber Park, Nottinghamshire, England. These Spaniels are one of the quieter hunting dogs. They are powerful and devoted dogs.

36. Cocker Spaniel
Puppy Eyes. Cocker Spaniel's have excellent hunting skills for flushing and retrieving bird and small game. They are good with children, cheerful, bright and an all around lovable pet.

37. Collie
Lassie. Because of its heritage, this dog is also known as the

Scottish Collie. They were developed as working dogs, and moved livestock. They are a beautiful and friendly breed.

38. Coonhound, Black & Tan
The Bear Dog. Coonhounds have a strong scent instinct. They have been used to hunt bear, deer and mountain lion, and bark when their quarry is in a tree. They are playful, fun dogs.

39. Coton de Tulear
Madagascar Royalty. Coton is the French word for cotton, and describes this breed's cottony coat. Cotons love to play, swim and jump on their hind legs. They are happy and gentle.

40. Curly-Coated Retriever
The Curly-Q Retriever. This breed is an excellent water retriever. Their coat is unique and weather resistant. They are faithful and devoted family members.

41. Dachshund
Hotdog. Dachshunds were bred in Germany during the 16th century, to hunt foxes and rabbits. Their long body allowed them to chase prey underground. They are tireless and clever.

42. Dalmatian
The Firehouse Dog. The Dalmatian is thought to have originated in Northern India, where the breed was used as a sentry. They are quick, loving and dedicated dogs.

43. Dandie Dinmont Terrier
The Biggest Little Dog. The Dandie Dinmont is one of the oldest British terriers. They are longer than they are tall. They are independent, lively, persistent and friendly.

44. Dingo
The Aborigine. The Dingos descendants are the last living link between the wolf and the domestic dog. A pure Dingo is scarce, and interbreeding is illegal. They are smart and curious.

45. Doberman Pinscher
The Army Dog. Doberman's are known for their devotion to duty on the German front during World War I. They are consistently on alert, and are proud and noble.

46. Dogo Argentino
The Fearless Hunter. This breed was developed in the 1920's in Argentina to be a big game hunter, family guardian, military and police dog. They are dependable and playful.

47. English Foxhound
The Elegant Hound. Breeding several different hounds together developed the English Foxhound. This hearty hound loves to run. They are obedient and have excellent stamina.

48. English Springer Spaniel
The Ancient Spaniel. The English Springer Spaniel thrives on the pursuit of game. Their primary purpose was to "spring" the quarry from their hiding places. They are friendly and devoted.

49. German Shepherd
The Guard Dog. German Shepherds work well as police, guide or search and rescue dogs. This breed deeply bonds with its family. They are very dependable and faithful.

50. German Shorthaired Pointer
The Noble Hunter. On land or icy water, the German Shorthaired Pointer can trail, point and retrieve. They are excellent watchdogs and reliable with children.

51. Golden Retriever
The Helper. Golden Retrievers can hunt on land and in water, and are used as guide dogs due to their intelligence and trainability. Golden Retrievers are loving and good-natured.

52. Great Dane
Apollo. In their native land of Germany, this breed was used to

hunt boar. Due to their large size, they need lots of room to play and run. They are protective, courageous and friendly.

53. Great Pyrenees
The Wise One. In the Pyrenees Mountains of France and Spain, these dogs, protected sheep, goats and cattle from wolves and bears. They are calm, patient, dependable dogs.

54. Greater Swiss Mountain Dog
The Swissy. Descendent from Roman Mastiffs, Swissy's were used in steep mountain villages of Switzerland for herding and guard dogs. They are bold, alert, loving and protective.

55. Greyhound
The Fastest Dog. This breed was developed as a sight hound for hunting, but is now known as a racing dog. They have a natural affinity for running and chasing objects. Greyhounds are friendly, obedient and good-natured.

56. Havanese
The Cuban National Dog. This breed is named after the Cuban city of Havana. It's believed that at one time the only way to own this gorgeous dog was to receive one as a good luck gift or gratitude gift. They are friendly, cheerful and obedient.

57. Ibizan Hound
The Brave Hunter. The Ibizan Hound is an old hunting breed from the Island of Ibiza, off the coast of Spain. They have a highly developed sense of smell, sight and hearing. They are loving, calm, kind and caring.

58. Irish Setter
Big Red. The Irish Setter has endless stamina, and is a little lighter and faster than other setters. On the field, they are fast and tough bird dogs. At home they are friendly and playful.

59. Irish Wolfhound
The Perfect Gentleman. The Irish Wolfhound is so tall that if it were standing on its hind legs could reach close to seven feet high. They are bright and easy to train.

60. Jack Russell
Eddie (from the television show Frasier). A clergyman named John Russell developed the Jack Russell in 19th century Devonshire, England. Originally they were used to hunt fox and small game. They are perky, fearless, playful and clever.

61. Japanese Chin
The Majestic One. This breed's exact beginning is a mystery, but one theory is that they originated in Korea then Japan then later in Europe. They were highly prized, and given to royalty as gifts. They are a charming, happy, kind and devoted dog.

62. Komondor
The Reggae Dog. During World War II, Komondors guarded military installations in Hungary. They're covered with a heavy, white-corded coat. They are very strong and agile.

63. Kuvasz
The Original. The Kuvasz can be traced as far back as 1342 in Hungary. They were used as guard dogs and for hunting. They are best as a one-family dog, and are extremely obedient.

64. Labrador Retriever
Loyal Pal. With no effort the Labrador Retriever can go from the show ring to the hunting field to home. They are strong and very active dogs. Labs are reliable and hardworking.

65. Lhasa Apso
The Earliest Sentry. Originating in the villages near Lhasa, Tibet the Lhasa was bred to guard monasteries and homes of high-ranking officials. The breed has a smart, sixth sense to tell friend from foe.

66. Maltese
The Gorgeous One. There are paintings and art objects of Maltese dating back 3,000 years. They have a long, white coat that requires frequent grooming. They are playful and devoted.

67. Mastiff
Home Body. Mastiffs are massive in size, and mainly used for protection and guardian dogs. They stay close to home, and are not likely to roam. Mastiffs are dignified and loving.

68. Miniature Schnauzer
The Lap Dog. This breed originated in Germany, and was originally used to hunt vermin, but is now mostly a companion dog. They are perky, playful, loving and faithful.

69. Newfoundland
The Lifeguard. The Newfoundland has webbed feet, and is an excellent swimmer and even known to rescue drowning victims. They are immensely devoted and protective breed.

70. Norwegian Elkhound
The Gentle Giant. The Norwegian Elkhound has the courage and stamina to hold big game at a distance. They have the endurance to track for hours, and in all types of weather and terrain. They make an excellent guardian and family member.

71. Otterhound
The Lover. The Otterhound is a large, rough-coated hound with great strength and dignity. They have an extremely sensitive nose. This dog makes an excellent family companion.

72. Papillon
The French Butterfly. The word Papillon means butterfly. When their ears are up their long, silky, fringed hair and heads resemble a butterfly. They are sweet, gentle and graceful.

73. Pharaoh Hound
The Ancient Egyptian. Historians believe the ancient Egyptian god, Anubis, was modeled after the Pharoah Hound. They were thought to speak for the gods. This breed can smile and blush. They are devoted, dependable and love to play.

74. Pekingese
The Shaman. There's a tale that these dogs are a pint size version of the ancient Chinese Foo Dogs, and keep evil spirits away. Royalty pampered this breed for centuries in China. They are calm, affectionate and devoted.

75. Pomeranian
Spunky. Some believe Pomeranian's are descendants of the sled dogs of Iceland. The breed originated in an area of Germany called Pomeranian, which is located on the southern coast of the Baltic Sea. They are smart and happy dogs.

76. Plott
The Hardiest Hound. In 1750, the Plott was used for boar hunting in Germany. They have an uncommon sharp, high-pitched bark. They are steadfast, intelligent and courageous.

77. Polish Lowland Sheepdog
Shaggy. Polish Lowlands were developed in central Asia to herd animals. They make excellent guard and watchdogs. They have a good memory, are even-tempered and lively.

78. Poodle
Circus Dog. The Poodle is a long time favorite in France, where they originated. Initially they were used to aid hunters and retrieve waterfowl. They are clever and easily trained.

79. Portuguese Water Dog
The Water Dog. They are exceptional swimmers and divers, and were used to retrieve broken fishing nets or carry messages from boat to shore. Water Dogs are smart and active.

80. Pug
Temple Dog. Pugs began as guard dogs in ancient Chinese temples. After saving the life of William, Prince of Orange, in 1572, the pug became the official dog of the House of Orange in Holland. They are playful, out-going and loveable.

81. Puli
The Springy Mop. They were used as police dogs in Hungary. Due to the unusual cording of their hair, a daily grooming is required. The Puli learn quickly, and are loving, curious dogs.

82. Redbone Coonhound
Expert Hunter. Redbone Coonhounds are able to tree coons fast, and are good at tracking bears, cougar and bobcat. They are strong, quick and have a pleasant bark.

83. Rhodesian Ridgeback
The Braided Dog. The Rhodesian Ridgeback is a native of South Africa. They have a unique ridge on their back from hair growing in the opposite direction to the rest. They are quiet, have a gentle temperament and rarely bark.

84. Rottweiler
The Natural Protector. Originally used as a herder, the Rottweiler quickly became better known as a guard dog. They are generally quiet, fearless, alert and steadfast.

85. Saint Bernard
The Savior. In the 17th century, monks of the Hospice of Saint Bernard in the Swiss Alps used these dogs as mountain guides, search and rescue, and for their ability to predict avalanches. If trained well they can be gentle, loving watchdogs.

86. Saluki
Egyptian Royalty. Ancient Egyptian Pharaohs hunted with a hawk on their wrist and a Saluki by their side. Egyptians even mummified their Salukis. They are devoted dogs that expect to be pampered.

87. Samoyed
Teddy Bear. The Samoyed is one of the purest breeds. The Samoyed people used them as sled and guard dogs. They are good-natured, mischievous and loyal.

88. Scottish Deerhound
Scotland Royalty. The Scottish Deerhound is a descendant of ancient greyhounds that were companions to the Celts. They are quiet, loving and have an easy-going manner.

89. Shetland Sheepdog
Scottish Shepherd. This breed was named after the Shetland Islands, located off the cold coast of Scotland. They were used to herd flocks of sheep. Shelties are dependable and obedient.

90. Shiba Inu
Mr. Clean. Originating in Japan, the Shiba Inu was used to hunt small animals and birds. They clean themselves like a cat, and can climb. They are active and faithful.

91. Shih Tzu
The Gift. Their exact origin is debated, but they are in paintings dated from the sixteenth century. They were given as gifts for good luck. They are gentle, playful and friendly.

92. Siberian Husky
Iditarod Master. The Chukchi nomads used the Siberian Husky to pull sleds and herd reindeer in the Tundra regions of Northeastern Siberia. They are dependable and smart dogs.

93. Silky Terrier
Feisty Friend. The Silky is named after their long, luxuriant hair coat. They were developed in Australia by breeding several different terriers together. They are spunky and sweet.

94. Tibetan Mastiff
The Monk. These Mastiff's protected livestock and villages

in their native Tibet. They need a lot of exercise and regular grooming. They are loving, gentle and protective.

95. Tibetan Spaniel
The Magi. In Tibet, this dog was only given as a gift. In ancient times, their keen sense of sight was used to patrol the walkways and monasteries. They are happy and bright.

96. Tibetan Terrier
Good Luck Charm. This breed comes from the Lost Valley of Tibet, an area so remote in the Himalayan Mountains of Asia that visitors used these dogs on their journeys. They look like miniature sheepdogs. They are smart, happy and loving dogs.

97. Toy American Eskimo
The Fluffball. The Eskie is an excellent watchdog. They have a fluffy, white, thick coat that needs regular grooming. They are a hardy breed, that is devoted, charming and kind.

98. Toy Fox Terrier
Little Foxy. This breed was originally developed as a ratter, but now used mainly for companionship. They are a little calmer than other Fox Terriers. Toys are clever and alert.

99. Vizla
The Chameleon. Vizslas are powerful hunters, but loving at home. This Hungarian breed is a great jumper, and will easily escape from a low fence. They are reliable with children and will quickly adapt to family life.

100. Yorkshire Terrier
The Pampered Pooch. This breed is native to Yorkshire, England, and was developed from several different terriers. The Yorkie is one of the most popular toy breeds in many countries. They are fast learners, playful and devoted.

PAWS TOGETHER

Prayer

Now I lay me down to sleep
I turn in place and shuffle my feet
I lay on my side and hardly move
Then sink right into my usual groove.
No one disturbs me I must confide
Till morning comes and I bound outside.
So thank you lord for so generously
Giving me the best family
They hug and hold and squeeze me tight
And share their love with me for life.

Just in case you were curious what the author's scores are… Lori is a Yorkie, Shiba Inu, Brittany and a Beagle overall. Just for the record, Lori cheated BIG TIME to be a Yorkie. Tami is an Anatolian Shepherd, Mastiff, Greater Swiss Mountain Dog and an Akita overall.

For this book, we were only able to use one hundred breeds, and apologize if your dog was left out. Even though countless hours went into research for this book, it is not a scientific test. Each answer is open to interpretation. Quite a few breeds history are questionable, disputed or unknown. Many share the same personality, appearance or behavior. For the purpose of this book, only one trait out of many may have used in determining each question and answer rather than an entire breed profile. Be aware that as in any family there is that one individual that may not follow true to breed standard. A dog's upbringing or household, bloodline, and many other factors play a part in their general behavior.

www.ingramcontent.com/pod-product-compliance
Lightning Source LLC
Chambersburg PA
CBHW060849050426
42453CB00008B/918